The Laugavegur Trail
A Hiking Companion to Iceland's Famous Trek

Brian W. Zimmer

CONTENTS

ACKNOWLEDGMENTS

I would like to thank the Appalachian State University Geology Department for their support of my work in Iceland. I would also like to thank all the students and colleagues who have accompanied me on these trips. Your collective curiosity, personality, and intelligence make each trip more colorful and engaging. Thanks to my folks, Chris and Larry Zimmer, for guidance and support. Finally, thanks to Meg. Though I am excited to go to Iceland each year, I am just as happy to return home to our life together.

Preface

The wonder of Iceland is something that everyone should have the opportunity to experience at some point in their life. By picking up this guide, you have already taken the first step. Due to the remote nature of the island, Iceland has long been an expensive place to holiday, but as part of the recovery from the economic collapse of 2008-2011, vacationing in Iceland is now more reasonable, though still slightly more expensive than much of Europe. Since the crisis, Iceland has embraced tourism and enhanced the services available.

The Laugavegur trail is the crown jewel backpacking trek in Iceland due to its beauty and accessibility. The Laugavegur is a festival of colors and sensations. You climb into snow-packed peaks, descend into verdant valleys, cross barren deserts and explore vents of recent volcanic eruptions. It is a great cross-section of the myriad of geologic and environmental settings found on the island, all on a single 5-day trek.

A mediocre band once crooned, "Call a place paradise, kiss it goodbye". Whether you like the Eagles or not, you have to acknowledge their warning. All too often we travel to beautiful places and we consume, discard, trample, and otherwise degrade them through our presence. As visitors, we are under every obligation to be stewards of the land and protect Iceland's valuable natural resources. Leave-no-trace practices are a must. This means that we must pack out all our rubbish, tread lightly on the fragile mosses, and reject the temptation to poach campsites. In this way, we assure that those who follow us to Iceland are afforded a spectacular wilderness and great adventures.

Spring 2014   Brian Zimmer

Using This Guide

This guide is meant to help you plan, prepare, and enjoy your trek on the Laugavegur Trail. As a volcanologist, I have great interest in the many volcanic centers passed on the trek and the stories they tell. My goal is to share those stories with you and to provide geologic context through anecdotal observations and annotated panoramas. I try to keep the jargon to a minimum, but some terminology is quite useful and all *italicized* words can be found in the glossary section at the back of the guide. In addition, crude translations of many Icelandic words are also located in the back of the guide. This guide is best used in conjunction with the 1:100,000 Serkort #4 map (Landmannalaugar, Þórsmörk, and Fjallabak) available at the BSI bus station in Reykjavik and online (http://www.forlagid.is). This journey is yours, so make it so. My recommendations are just that, recommendations. Do not limit yourself by what is written here, but rather use it as a launching point for your own adventures.

Pre-Departure Considerations

Food and Supplies

Most people will fly in and out of Keflavik airport. The nearest city to Keflavik is Reykjavik, home to about 2/3 of Iceland's total population. In Reykjavik, there are several shopping options for food and supplies. Food can be purchased all around Reykjavik at Bónus, Krónan, Nettó, 10-11, or various other stores. Bónus and 10-11 stores are in closest proximity to the city center and the BSI bus terminal where most people arrive from the airport and where tour buses depart to points all over Iceland. Bónus tends to be larger and more modestly priced than 10-11, though the 10-11 does offer high-quality bulk items like

> ## Economics
> Icelandic economics are simple. If you are shopping for a necessity that Icelanders use regularly, you can find it and it will be fairly priced. If you are looking for luxury items or experiences (i.e. eating out, ear plugs, ice cream, freeze-dried meals), you will pay dearly for them, if you can find them at all.

yogurt-covered raisins or chocolate-covered pretzels. Krónan and Nettó stores are similar to Bónus and can be found in other parts of Reykjavik and smaller towns around Iceland.

If you prefer spending money and saving weight, a variety of freeze-dried breakfasts and dinners are available at Fjallakofinn in the Kringlan shopping center. Expect to pay a lot for these convenient meals. I'm too frugal to purchase these meals myself, but a colleague of mine purchased them last year and was quite pleased with the results. Be sure to add the water slowly and mix thoroughly to better hydrated the chicken croutons and incorporated all the spices that usually get stuck in the package corners. Fjallakofinn is the REI / Dick's sporting goods of Iceland and I have been thankful for its existence. One year, I strapped my tent poles to the outside of my pack during the flight over. Bad idea. My bag arrived but the poles were gone. I was able to hike over to Fjallakofinn and get a bomb-proof caterpillar-shaped tent for a reasonable price.

Gas for cook stoves is readily available in Iceland. The most common type available is the Primus canister with the threaded tip. These are interchangeable with MSR canisters commonly found in the US and elsewhere and are available at most gas stations / convenience stores, especially in towns where there are developed campgrounds. I've found that the gas stations in immediate proximity to Keflavik airport sell cooking gas for about twice the price elsewhere in the country. White gas is also widely available.

If you forgot any crucial equipment, like your cook set, sleeping pad, or your *ahem* tent poles and don't want to pony up to buy replacements, you can always rent equipment through *Iceland Camping Equipment* (www.iceland-camping-equipment.com). The store is located about 1km north of the BSI station. I have rented from them before and have been satisfied with their equipment and prices.

Money

Iceland's currency is the Icelandic Krona. The currency is commonly abbreviated by either ISK or Kr. Coins come in 1, 10, 50, and 100 denominations; bank notes are in denominations of 500kr, 1,000kr, 2,000kr, and 5,000kr. Due to the dynamic nature of the Icelandic economy over the last few years, I will not even endeavor to suggest what an exchange rate would be. Let it simply be said that the rate is highly variable. Cash exchange booths are located within Keflavik airport and ATMs are common in Reykjavik and most towns with grocery stores, gas stations, or banks. Landsbanki Íslands is the most common provider of banking and ATM services and their ATMs accept Cirrus and Plus cards along with all major debit and credit cards. Credit cards provide reasonable exchange rates and are widely accepted in towns, though be aware that most banks now charge a 1-3% "foreign transaction fee" for each purchase. On the trail, you will want to bring cash to pay for your sleeping accommodations. The rangers appreciate it when you have smaller bills, as maintaining a large supply of change can be difficult for them.

Maps and GPS

There are at least two good maps that show the Laugavegur trail and surrounding areas in reasonable detail. The aforementioned and recommended Serkort #4 map (Landmannalaugar, Þórsmörk, and Fjallabak) can be purchased on the internet (www.omnimap.com/catalog/int/iceland.htm#p 9 or www.forlagid.is) and is available at the BSI station, tourist stores in Reykjavik and some of the well-stocked campground stores across the country. The Serkort map shows the entire length of the trail in 1:100,000 ratio scale and the greater

Þórsmörk area in 1:50,000 ratio scale. The 1:100,000 scale does not provide quite enough detail to really track your every move on the trail, but it is very good for identifying major stream crossings, trail junctions, and the names of surrounding peaks. My first year hiking the Laugavegur trail (2008), I bought a smaller map called *Landmannalaugar for Hikers* from the supply bus in Landmannalaugar which had better detail, but less regional context. I have not found that map for sale anywhere else in Iceland and according to the supply bus's website, it is no longer published. The routes have been altered slightly, but if you can find it, buy it. I believe it was the higher-detail (1:50,000) for the entire trail.

GPS units work well in Iceland due to the open, treeless terrain. My preference is to keep a GPS unit on me, but to use it only in case of emergency or to mark sample collection sites. Even very basic GPS units have a "backtrack" function that will help guide you back to a starting point, which can be critical if weather kicks up or if you get disoriented in a snowfield. All things considered, the Laugavegur pathway is well marked and well-traveled. GPS units are generally not necessary, as long as you bring your common sense along.

Best Time of Year

The Laugavegur trail is only passable a few months out of the year. Melting snow gives way in late June, allowing access to those taking public transport. Along the trail, you will have the choice of camping or staying in huts. The huts open around June 25th each year, though conditions change and you should personally check the accessibility if you are planning on an early-season trek. Throughout July and early August, the trail sees the most hikers. By mid-August the numbers tail off and the weather gets a bit cooler and wetter. I have hiked as late as August 18th. We had the trail almost to ourselves, but we also caught a blizzard in the highlands. By the 1st or 2nd week of September the huts close and bus service ends.

Dangers

Safety is obviously of paramount concern when you are out hiking in an area as remote as the volcanic highlands of Iceland. The Laugavegur Trail does not skirt many cliff edges or cross crevasse-strewn glaciers, but you must retain a level of self-sufficiency and common sense as you explore. Hypothermia can be a concern and, time and again, I have realized that there is no such thing as bad weather, just bad equipment. Worse than snow is a cold, soaking rain. Your rain gear should be high-quality. Don't risk your safety and comfort by bringing only a poncho or one of those thin yellow fisherman outfits that split the moment you try to squat in it. You need a solid shell and durable, waterproof pants.

River crossings are invigorating but must be approached with caution. Just because it says there is a river crossing in the guide, it does not mean that the river is passable at all times. After rain storms or in the midst of spring runoff, the rivers can flow at much higher rates, putting you at greater risk.

Only you can decide what is safe for you. When crossing rivers, you should put on designated "river shoes". **Do not cross barefoot!** These shoes can be old sneakers or strap-on sandals. Flip flops will be torn from your feet and end up deposited in the North Atlantic. Unbuckle your pack and face slightly upstream as you make your way across the river. Many hikers use trekking poles. I prefer to link arms or clasp wrists with fellow hikers for support if the water is knee deep or greater. No matter how deep it is, it will be cold (3-5° C), so do not dally in the river for long.

Gray clays indicating hydrothermal alteration

Particular care should be taken in the geothermal areas including the hotsprings, *fumaroles,* and recent *lava* flows. The hot spring at Landmannalaugar is safe to bathe in, but elsewhere on the trail, assume that the bubbling springs are at or near boiling. Please, do not reach out a hand to test. Around many of the *fumaroles,* or steam jets, you will see grey to white hydrothermally altered clays. This land is not stable and is susceptible to collapse or at least sinking of a foot into a hot acidic mud bath. Enjoy the jets, take some pictures, but there is little reason for detailed inspection that involves your face or hand within spatter distance of a volcanic conduit.

Should you find yourself badly injured, dialing 112 will get you in contact with Icelandic emergency assistance. In urbanized areas, dialing 1770 will call a doctor to your location. Cell coverage in Iceland is excellent. This link:

http://www.vodafone.is/internet/farnet/utbreidsla/ provides a map of coverage as of 2014. Most of the trail has coverage and if you are in a dark area, climbing a ridge will usually get you signal. Cell phones that work in Iceland can be rented through Iceland Camping Equipment as well (www.iceland-camping-equipment.com). Incoming calls are free. The level of care available in Reykjavik is excellent, though rural areas have lower capabilities. Most major injuries are treated in Reykjavik, if transport is an option. On the trail, you are never more than 10km from a warden's hut and many times you are much closer than that. Wardens are able to arrange medical evacuations and some level of care, but their services should only be used in **emergencies**.

Hiking Times

The hiking times suggested in this guide are based on reasonable weather and a pleasant, but certain forward pace. Your time will vary depending on your goals, susceptibility to photogenic diversions, and conditioning. On most days, you will have 20+ hours of sunlight to hike 10-15km. Some folks will want to bang out the hike in the morning and then rest or day hike around the day's destination. Others will meander through the trail, stopping often, exploring side trails, and taking pictures. Use whatever pace works for you. There is no real difference between arriving at 2PM and 9PM. The important thing is that you hike it exactly as you please.

Choosing a Direction

For me, the decision to hike south from Landmannalaugar is simply one of aesthetics, comfort, and logistics. Your needs and desires may be much different, but for those of you looking for a recommendation, here is mine. I bring 10-15 university-aged geology students to Iceland with me each year to hike the Laugavegur trail. Traveling south, our first night at Hrafntinnusker is generally the coldest. It is best to get this out of the way early so the students are not dreading the looming "cold" night. Sometimes, it is quite nice up there, but more often than not, it can be challenging; especially the wind. However, the struggle of the first night makes day 2, when you break out over Jökultungur and overlook the green Álftavatn valley, that much more spectacular.

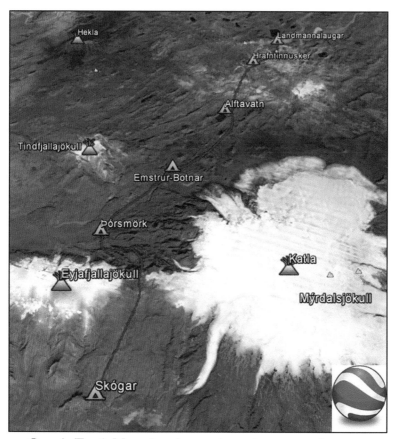

Google Earth Map showing major volcanoes and camps

There is also the comfort factor of the prevailing wind direction. During the summer, the wind tends to blow from north to south until you get to Þórsmörk, where you begin to be influenced by coastal wind patterns and the direction is move variable. Hiking southward ensures that you will not eat as much grit walking through the *basalt* desert between Álftavatn and Emstrur and, if a storm does blow up, it will be at your back, pushing you forward instead of soaking your face.

Hiking south also lets you day hike from Þórsmörk up to the new vents atop Fimmvörðuháls without having to go all the way to Skógar. This is what I commonly do with my students if they are not up for the full 25 km stretch. We get up early, day-hike to the vents and are back in time to catch the afternoon bus from Þórsmörk to Reykjavik. Most hikers on the Laugavegur trail travel from north to south. During high season, about 100 people begin the hike each day. Heading south, you can choose to hike with a group, or wait 10 minutes and have relative solitude, even during peak times.

There are some advantages to hiking the opposite direction: South to North. First and foremost, you will end your trip at Landmannalaugar where you can rest your aching self in the hot spring. Northbound hikers will see the trail as fewer people have and your pictures will no doubt be different. You will see a constant trickle of hikers throughout the day and this can be good, bad, or inconsequential depending on your desire for solitude versus social opportunities. Though both directions have their merits, for the remainder of this guide we will discuss the trail as though you are hiking the more common route of north to south, Landmannalaugar to Þórsmörk, or Skógar.

Getting There

In years past, hikers had fewer options to get out to Landmannalaugar or Þórsmörk. Private vehicles, hitch-hiking, or catching one of the early, infrequent tour buses were the primary options. With the rebound of Iceland's tourist industry and the growing popularity of the Laugavegur Trail, tour companies, especially Reykjavik Excursions, have stepped up and provide ample, regular public transportation to the major access points on the trail.

Even if your bus catches a flat, rescue buses are immediately dispatched, keeping you on schedule.

Today, you can catch a morning bus from the BSI station near the city center in Reykjavik to Landmannalaugar, Þórsmörk, or Skógar for a hefty, but not unreasonable price. At the time of writing, the buses run from June to mid-September, once a day to Landmannalaugar, twice to Þórsmörk and twice a day to Skógar. The best deal for folks wanting to hike the Laugavegur trail is to use the "Hiking Passport". This is a bus pass that allows you to travel one-way to or from any of the three aforementioned access points. This means it will work if you are traveling north or south on the trail and you can even add on hiking the Fimmvörðuháls pass at no extra charge. It is substantially cheaper than buying two one-way tickets. Reservations and scheduling details are available via the Reykjavik Excursions website: www.re.is.

If you take one of the Reykjavik Excursion busses, you will hear a delightfully Icelandic explanation of regional geology and culture along the bus route from Reykjavik to Landmannalaugar. By "delightfully Icelandic", I mean it is like a kind and wise man sat down with a recorder and simply started talking about life in Iceland without a script of any sort. It is very refreshing and ultimately enlightening and entertaining. Another bonus of taking the bus is that you will stop at an overlook where you can gaze upon the snow-covered and often cloud-shrouded summit of Hekla volcano.

> ## A Note on Hitch-hiking
>
> **While Iceland is a very safe and hitch-hiker-friendly country, one should be somewhat wary about attempting to hitch to Landmannalaugar. During my journeys, I have picked up many hitch-hikers who report that their longest waits have been on the way out to Landmannalaugar. If you are very flexible, this potential delay may not be a problem, but you could go several hours to even days waiting for a ride. There is little traffic on the track, and those vehicles that do come by are usually already full of people and gear or are tour buses. You might get lucky and catch a ride quickly, but take this word of caution seriously if you are constrained by time.**

Hekla (1,488 meters)

In Icelandic, the word "hekla" is used to describe a small, hooded cloak; an appropriate name for a volcano whose summit is so often obscured by clouds. Hekla is a stratovolcano, meaning that it has been formed over thousands of years through both explosive eruptions that produce lots of *pyroclastic* material and *effusive* eruptions that produce significant volumes of *lava*. A unique geologic aspect of Hekla is that it is generally aseismic, meaning that it does not experience regular earthquakes except in the hours and minutes immediately preceding an eruption. For most volcanoes, there is a ramping up of seismicity over the course of several weeks leading up to an eruption. Aseismic eruptions are not fair. It would be like a shark attacking without having the common courtesy to play the JAWS theme for at least a minute beforehand.

Christians of the middle ages believed Hekla was the "Gateway to Hell". During eruptions, people would see the volcanic *bombs* and other projectiles flying away from the glowing crater and interpret these to be human souls. The hissing sounds the *bombs* made as they flew were interpreted to be the screams of the damned. The rocky spires and erosional remnants around Hekla sometimes take on almost human shapes and give rise to myths of Ice Trolls guarding the volcano's slopes.

Other Christian accounts suggest that Hekla was the home of Judas. As I recall, Judas lived in warmer climates, but regardless… Folks aren't being unjustly grim in their appraisals of Hekla. Throughout recorded history, Hekla has been a feisty beast, having significant eruptions on average about every 50 years. Recently, Hekla has been even more active; erupting every

Hekla on a cloudy day in 2008

10 years or so with the most recent eruption in 2000. If you feel so inclined, you can hike to the summit and ski around the crater rim or take a snow cat up in the winter time. Just be sure to know your escape routes and tread cautiously if you go on Easter because that is when witches are reported to gather on Hekla's slopes to perform their nefarious incantations.

Fjallabak Nature Reserve

The common starting point for a southbound journey on the Laugavegur trail is Landmannalaugar. Landmannalaugar is both the base camp for the trail and a destination in of itself. It is located within the Fjallabak Nature Reserve; an area of desolate and wild beauty. The reserve is over 47,000 hectares and is home to many volcanoes, geothermal hot springs, lakes, and rivers as well as a fine variety of vegetation and wildlife. Ólafur Örn Haraldsson has written a thorough guide to the reserve simply named: *Fjallabak Nature Reserve.* The book is not widely available, but can be purchased in most bookshops in Reykjavik. While hiking the Laugavegur trail, your first day and a half will be spent within the reserve before exiting just south of Hrafntinnusker. Wilderness camping is not permitted within the reserve, but there are several designated campgrounds at Landmannahellir, Hrafntinnusker, and the main one at Landmannalaugar.

Vegetation

While in the reserve and for much of the trail, you will be surrounded by colorful, yet delicate alpine wildflowers, such as cottongrass (Eriophorum angustifolium), sea thrift (Armeria maritime), wood crane's bill (Geranium sylvaticum), creeping thyme (Thymus praecox), and sea campion (Silene uniflora). As with any delicate ecosystem, the wildflowers are best viewed and photographed, but not picked.

During late summer, the valleys surrounding Landmannalaugar are blanketed with cottongrass. Cottongrass seeds and stems are edible and the leaves and roots have been used traditionally for medicinal purposes due to their astringent properties. Contrary to what its name would have you believe, the white tufts do not spin well into thread, though they have been used for candle wicks, dressings for wounds, and pillow stuffing.

Cottongrass (Eriophorum angustifolium)

Sea campion will be a constant companion throughout the hike, especially in the well-drained soils of the *basalt* flats between Álftavatn and Emstrur. Look, but do not pick it, because A) you shouldn't pick any wildflowers and B) sea campion is also known as "Dead man's bells" or "Devil's hatties". Picking it tempts death, according to Icelandic tradition.

Sea Campion (Silene uniflora)

Trees are very rare in Iceland. When settlement began around 870 AD, about 25% of the land area of Iceland was covered in forest. Within a few decades, 80% of the timber had been removed for pasture or building materials. Today, only 1% of Iceland's landmass remains forested. This was not the result of aggressive, careless exploitation of resources, but rather was a result of early settlers not understanding the fragility of the environment they had moved into. Their practices were relatively sustainable for hundreds of years in Norway and northern Britain, but the highly erosive environment and slow rates of soil development and vegetation growth led to Iceland becoming more barren. Today, the remaining forests are well managed and protected. They comprise stands of northern birch, aspen, rowan, juniper, and spruce. On the Laugavegur trail trees are absent entirely until you drop down toward Þórsmörk and the stunted birch that fill the valley there.

Wildlife

Mammals are not very common in Iceland simply due to their high caloric demands and the paucity of readily available calories. Much of the land in Iceland is essentially barren; glaciers cover 11% of the total land area while lava fields and deserts cover another 60%. The arctic fox is the only native land mammal. It is found within Fjallabak though I have not yet sighted one. Other mammals present in Iceland include non-native species, such as mink, mice, and reindeer. Birds are also not particularly common, but you may see ptarmigan or falcons within the reserve. A few song birds live in the forests near Þórsmörk.

Landmannalaugar

Welcome to Landmannalaugar! This tent city is the launching point for your upcoming adventure. Landmannalaugar's campground is often packed with colorful tents, colorful characters, and the quiet murmur of a dozen different languages. Do not be alarmed by the large population. Many folks are here for the day to hike one of many nearby trails. In terms of amenities, the campground boasts a large bathroom and shower facility and a sheltered cooking area, complete with picnic tables and sinks for washing dishes. There is also a 110 bed tourist hut operated by Ferdafelag Islands. Reservations are strongly recommended during peak summer travel periods. No reservations are required for camping.

Arriving in Landmannalaugar, one is presented with two options. If the weather is pleasant, you can register with the park warden and leave directly for Hrafntinnusker. Many folks, looking for reprieve from the bustle of Landmannalaugar, begin the hike immediately. If you are not in a rush, I highly recommend taking the rest of your travel day to explore the area surrounding Landmannalaugar and begin the Laugavegur trail in the morning. If you decide to hit the trail, you will have to register at the warden's hut. If you are camping, you will also have to visit the hut to pay for your overnight accommodations.

The wardens are very helpful, but also very busy when busses arrive and a rush of hikers all try to register at once. If you give it an hour, things are much more relaxed. The wardens are a wealth of readily-shared information, except if you ask them about the weather. Nobody wants to try to predict the weather. If a storm is coming in, they will certainly let you know, but they will never tell you that it will be sunny all day.

Fjallafang; Go for the scone!

Since the early 1990's a couple from Vestfirðir has been driving up one or two green busses full of supplies for Landmannalaugar travelers. The bus-shop is called *Fjallafang* and offers a wide variety of necessities and treats. Rain gear, boot laces, and first aid supplies are all available along with sweets, hot drinks, and dried fish. Surprisingly, they offer reasonably priced sandwiches ($3-$5 as of 2013). www.landmannalaugar.info/index.htm. Their website is worth a stop for lots of Landmannalaugar information and literary gems like this:

"Smokers can ceep (sic) their bad habits, but tobacco is expensive in our shop. They can try nose-tobacco for a change, we also have that."

And, "To avoid boredom in rainy days, our customers can buy postcards, candles, playing-cards and condoms."

Like everywhere along the Laugavegur, the weather in Landmannalaugar is highly dynamic and sometimes a fierce wind can kick up. In these instances, bent tent stakes barely driven into the rocky ground will not suffice. There are wooden crates containing large rocks around the campground to help hold down tents. Feel free to use them, but take the time to place the rocks back in the crates when you leave.

One of the highlights of spending an evening in Landmannalaugar is watching the sun set while sitting in the hot pools that are located a short walk north of the shower facility. Landmannalaugar literally means "the people's pools." Hot and cold springs mix along a small tributary, but certain areas maintain a very pleasant 36-40°C. It is fun to watch people scramble around trying to find the correct balance of temperature. The area surrounding the pools is a delicate bog, so do your best to stay on the wooden boardwalk. The pool can get crowded during peak times, but in the evening, when the day's visitors have left, the camp quiets down and you can have a calmer hot pool experience.

Landmannalaugar; looking back from Laugahraun

Day hikes

Taking the extra day in Landmannalaugar also offers you the opportunity to explore several excellent day hikes to whet your appetite for the upcoming journey. The following are a few favorite day hikes from the Landmannalaugar campground:

1. Bláhnúkur – Grænagil (2-3 hrs)
   This short, but steep hike will take you to the summit of Bláhnúkur (*Blue peak*), the relict edifice of a sub-glacial eruption during the last ice age (115-11ka; ka means kilo annus - 1000's of years ago). The hike begins south of the Landmannalaugar campground and climbs steeply to 360⁰ views at the summit (945m). You can take the same path straight back, or for a nice 6k loop, continue over the summit and turn right toward Grænagil (*Green gorge*). Follow the stream back toward camp.

Loop trail to the summit of Bláhnúkur. Trail begins just south of the Landmannalaugar campground

2. Jökulgil Valley (as much or little as you want!)
   The Jökulgil valley extends for over 13km southeast of Landmannalaugar. It is best enjoyed in the late summer or early fall when water levels have lowered and stream crossings are less arduous. The valley has been carved out by the annual runoff from

Torfajökull and the Reykja mountains and the views are truly spectacular. Generally, you will have the valley to yourself as well. The trail is the most eastern of the trails leading south from camp.

3. Brennisteinsalda Loop (1.5-5 hrs depending on the loop)
    This loop follows any of several different paths up Brennisteinsalda (861m). Brennisteinsalda means "sulfur wave" and is an appropriate name due to the presence of hot sulfur springs and vapor jets (*fumaroles*) coming off its flanks. Brennisteinsalda is a composition of many pastel colors mixing on its flanks and is perhaps the most photographed mountain in Iceland. From its summit you can look around 360⁰ and even see Hekla in the distance on clear days. This hike can be combined with a trip over Bláhnúkur for a nice 5 hr loop.

Brennisteinsalda as seen from Laugahraun lava flow

4. Suðurnámur to Vondugil and back through Laugahraun (3-4 hrs)
    This loop is just shy of 9km and walks the southern ridge of Suðurnámur (*Southern Quarry*). This is a *rhyolite* mountain that is approximately 200,000 years old. Get to the trail by walking north on the access road leading to Landmannalaugar. Stay left (south) and climb the ridge. From this ridge, you have a great view back on Landmannalaugar and Vondugil (*Wicked Valley*) immediately south.

The southern path is not particularly steep and the walking is relatively easy. Staying right at the start leads to the northern ridge as well as access to the Suðurnámur gorge that splits the mountain in two. From the southern trail, you can ford Námskvísl (*Wise River confluence*) in Vondugil and head back to the main path through the Laugahraun lava flow and ultimately end up back at camp.

History Bits

The Landmannalaugar area has long been used for sheep grazing, but historically, the Jokugil and Vondugil valleys were avoided during roundups due to the alleged presence of evil spirits. Any sheep that wandered into the valleys were abandoned and given up as lost. In 1852, the area was explored and mapped. With the exploration team reporting no mysterious events or features, farmers ventured into the valleys to retrieve their sheep and added the area back into their annual pasture.

Nína and Smári, the owners of the bus-shop, *Fjallafang,* created an artistic map and guide for many additional day-hikes that lead from Landmannalaugar campground. Their map is posted in their bus and is available for sale there. In recent years the hiking trails have been altered slightly and the map is not completely accurate.

Fishing licenses are available for purchase at the Landmannalaugar warden station for about $25. You get about $8 back if you turn in a fishing report at the end of your trip. Most of the glacial rivers you cross move too quickly for good fishing, but your second day of hiking ends at the picturesque mountain lake, Álftavatn. There are reports of char and lake trout in Álftavatn and no official daily limit. Use your own judgment. From Landmannalaugar, a short hike to the north will take you to Frostastaðavatn and some very decent fishing.

Day 1. Landmannalaugar – Hrafntinnusker
(12km; 4-5 hrs; Elevation gain 470m)

Much of the 1st day and part of the 2nd are spent within the Torfajökull *caldera*. *Calderas* are huge circular craters produced during the largest and most violent volcanic eruptions. The Torfajökull *caldera* is a modest 15km in diameter which is much smaller than other *calderas*, such as Yellowstone, which has an average diameter of around 63km. Though it is a relatively small *caldera*, Torfajökull is young, hot, and full of energy. The vitality of the *caldera* is expressed in the wide distribution of geothermal hot springs, mud

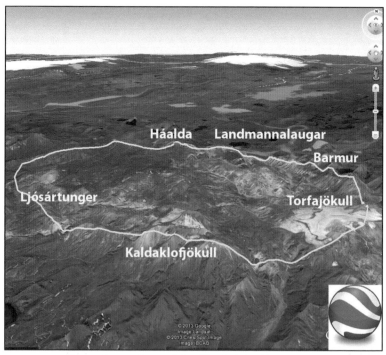

Rough outline of the Torfajökull caldera

pots, and *fumaroles*. You will see these throughout today's hike.

The Torfajökull *caldera* has been explored over the last 20 years in regard to its geothermal energy potential. The energy-generating potential is huge; around 1000MW, though there has been minimal development of the resource due to its remoteness. Throughout its eruptive history Torfajökull has produced both cataclysmic *caldera* eruptions (around 800,000 ybp) and *effusive* lava flows (8 flows in the last 11,500 years). The eruptive activity was a mix of sub-glacial eruptions varying in composition from *rhyolite* to *basalt*. Today, you can see many of the modern lava flows. In fact, the Laugavegur hike starts by crossing one of the recent Torfajökull flows, Laugahraun.

Cooled lava from the Laugahraun flow

In Icelandic, Laugahraun means "bathing lava;" a reference to the many thermal pools around the perimeter of the flow. The field is a *rhyolite* flow that was emplaced just inside the northern rim of the Torfajökull *caldera* during March of 1477. The 1477 eruption was a regional fissure eruption that also emplaced the Namshraun lava flow which is located just north of Landmannalaugar. The most recent eruption from the Torfajökull *caldera* was in 1480. The Laugahraun flow is little changed in the approximately 530 years since its emplacement except for the minor growth of mosses and lichens. The flow comprises a mixture of glassy *obsidian* and flow-banded *rhyolite*. *Obsidian* forms when lava cools extremely quickly; as when lava is emplaced into a lake, beneath a glacier or on top of snow. The flow banding within the lava is a result of ductile deformation that occurs as the high-viscosity lava begins to cool and shear.

If you look to the north as you cross the Laugahraun, you will see Suðurnámur, the split volcano mentioned on the page of recommended day hikes. The main trail turns south and skirts the flank of Brennisteinsalda (881m), one of Iceland's most colorful volcanic hills and the dominant peak rising southwest over Landmannalaugar campground. The colors of Brennisteinsalda are a result of hydrothermal alteration and oxidation of *felsic* minerals. Brennisteinsalda was, at least in part, formed during the same 1477-1480 eruptions that formed the Laugahraun lava flow. The lava flows and spires from this eruption are visible along the volcano's southern flank.

A short side trip can take you to the summit of Brennisteinsalda, where you can look east and see both Grænagil (Green Gorge) and Brennisteinsalda's sister mountain Bláhnúkur. Both Brennisteinsalda and Bláhnúkur show clear signs of being emplaced sub-glacially with an estimated ice thickness of almost 400m.

As the trail turns south, you are invited to gaze upon Vondugil (*Wicked Valley*). In mid-late summer the floor of the broad valley is covered by tundra cotton (*Eriophorum angustifolium*). The view is so pleasant and inviting, one wonders why early sheep herders thought the area home to evil spirits (see aforementioned "History Bits"). The area does call to you like a siren, begging you to wander up to the source of the Námskvísl. You can, should you feel so inclined, and you will have the valley to yourself except during the peak-most afternoons in late summer. One path leads up over Háalda. Háalda means "high smooth mountain" which is an appropriate name, if uncreative.

Continuing along the main path, you will pass a trail junction that will give you the option to double back through Grænagil and over to Landmannalaugar, but why would you want to bail now? We've only just begun!

The Laugavegur trail skirts and climbs along the flank of Brennisteinsalda, passing hot springs and *fumaroles*. As you skirt, looking east will give you an unobstructed view of the blue-hued scree slopes of Bláhnúkur's western amphitheater. The trail passes many lava domes and spires along Brennisteinsalda's eastern slope. Domes are plugs of viscous lava that are forced to the surface during *effusive* (non-explosive) phases of volcanic eruptions. Physically, there is little difference between a lava dome and a lava flow, except that the dome is a bit more viscous. Domes can vary in size from small blisters of a few cubic meters to much larger domes that are many cubic kilometers in volume. Keep this in mind as you will see some large-volume domes later today. The spires are erosional relicts left when the softer volcanics (all the colorful stuff) erode away, leaving behind the harder internal lava structures that acted as the plumbing for the volcano.

Leaving Brennisteinsalda behind, you will climb steadily for the next 2km. Your reward is the progressive reveal of a panorama to your left. The colorful *rhyolite* hills beneath Gráskalli (*Gray bald*) lay out before you; a patchwork quilt of snowpack, turf, and ash. The deeply incised drainages bear witness to the strong and active weathering forces at work. Streams of glacial runoff and snow melt easily remobilize the volcanics, cutting several cm deeper each year. Often fog can obscure this ridgeline, so if you are afforded the view on a clear day, such as the one I stumbled upon in 2013, count yourself among the lucky. The walking is rather easy through most of this section due to the soft nature of the sediments, but be aware that there are a few steep sections that can become quite slick when it is wet.

At a small plateau just beyond the panorama, the trail splits. The Laugavegur continues on toward the Stórihver hot springs while a side trail loops back over either Bláhnúkur or Skalli on a circuitous route back to Landmannalaugar. On clear days, from this plateau, you will begin to see the vast snowfields of the highlands and even catch your first glimpse of the glaciers Torfajökull and Kaldaklofsjökull (*Torfi's Glacier* and *Cold Straddling Glacier* respectively). The patchwork landscape reduces its pallet to mostly blacks, grays, and whites as the more colorful *rhyolites* are subdued beneath ash from the recent Eyjafjallajökull eruption (2010). The ash is not thick, but wind has distributed it widely and much of the snowpack looks smudged with soot.

Entering Storihver

The Stórihver hot spring area welcomes you with an embrace of sulfur-smelling mist. The smell is reminiscent of rotten eggs and is common to many volcanic areas. What you smell is the compound hydrogen sulfide (H_2S). This is produced when *magma* is degassing. The heat at Stórihver comes from *magma* bodies within the earth's crust that have found conduits through which gas and heat can escape to the surface. It reaches the surface as either dry, pressurized gas in the form of a *fumarole*, or it uses a pathway shared with water and emerges as a bubbling hot spring. On the large scale, monitoring hydrogen sulfide has been used with variable success as an indicator of increased volcanic activity. All active volcanoes degas some

H_2S. This is considered background. Significant spikes in H_2S compared to background levels may indicate that the *magma* has begun to mobilize and an eruption could be approaching. Hydrogen sulfide monitoring is just one aspect of volcano monitoring that is taken into consideration when making eruption forecasts.

Haalda Trail Junction

The deep green oasis of Stórihver makes for a pleasant resting location, especially when the weather is cold, just mind how many sulfurous clouds you huff while standing around. Sulfur concentrations in excess of 20ppm can cause significant eye and lung irritation. Extended exposure at 50ppm leads to irrecoverable eye damage and other unpleasant health issues. You will probably come nowhere close to these exposure levels in and around Stórihver, but if you start to feel eye or throat irritation, take it as a sign to move along. A trail junction here allows one to meet up with an alternate route to Stórihver via Háalda and Vondugil. Háalda, along with Suðurnámur mark the northern edge of the Torfajökull *caldera*.

Ash-covered highlands

Beyond Stórihver, the ground is predominantly covered by snow and ice, even during late July and early August. Fog and precipitation are also much more likely between Stórihver and Hrafntinnusker. Though the trail is clearly marked with tall wooden posts and rock cairns, caution must be exercised when weather does settle in. About 1 km from the Höskuldsskáli hut there is a memorial to a young Israeli who became disoriented on the trail and died during a summer blizzard. I tell this story not to make you fearful, but rather aware. Weather can shift on a dime. You will not be allowed out of the ranger station if you are wearing jeans (seriously). So be a Boy/Girl Scout; help old folks across the street, sell cookies, earn merit badges, and above all, be prepared for whatever weather comes your way.

Hrafntinnusker

I always get a surprisingly large wave of joy when I see the Höskuldsskáli hut at Hrafntinnusker. Perhaps I am far more tired than I am willing to admit. One starts to obsess, imagining that first cup of warm tea and chunk of chocolate. Traipse across the rolling hills to the hut and take a rest. Most folks stop here for the evening though some push on to the lower elevations of Álftavatn.

Höskuldsskáli hut sleeps about 36 people, most of whom are shoulder to shoulder on sleeping mats in an upstairs loft. The huts all along the trail are run by FÍ, an Icelandic hiking group. Generally, huts are cozy as opposed to crowded, but they can feel packed as everyone strips off wet clothing and tries to find an empty spot on the drying lines near the stove. It definitely gets crowded if campers try to wedge in and poach some drying space for clothing or cooking space. Campers are not allowed in the huts except in emergency situations. I have only stayed in the huts one time, but I've been on both sides of the issue; irritated by a few persistent trespassers and sitting wet and cold on the outside, wishing I had ponied up the extra cash so I could sip tea and read a book next to the fire. To be fair, the wardens do a good job of patrolling the huts and we campers are, by in large, content with our outdoor amenities.

Reservations are a must if you want a guaranteed spot in the hut. I got to try out the huts my first time out on the trail. A friend and I had just hiked in from Landmannalaugar in a cold, steady rain. We were soaked to the bone and really didn't want the trip starting off on a soggy note, so we checked with the ranger. Two beds had opened that day and we were luckily the first to try to claim them. Those same two free beds followed us the entire journey. A few days later, at Emstrur, a couple beat us to the beds. That evening was crystal clear and we camped happily.

At Hrafntinnusker, and everywhere else along the Laugavegur Trail, wilderness camping is prohibited. Designated campsites are about 100m down slope from the Höskuldsskáli hut. There are dry-stacked rock walls set up as wind breaks. These are invaluable and it is worth picking out the largest available wall to protect you from the prevailing winds. Nothing ruins a night's sleep like typhoon-strength winds pulling at your rain fly. Even if the evening looks clear when you set up, batten the hatches and stake everything down well. All campers have access to toilets and fresh-water sinks for drinking water and brushing teeth. There is a separate washing station for dishes. There is no rubbish collection at any of the huts so you must pack out all your trash.

Tents tucked in against stacked-rock wind breaks

Hrafntinnusker means *Obsidian* dome... roughly. Volcanic activity was centered here about 5000 BCE and the resulting eruption left behind a thick blanket of tephra and several small lava flows. The dome at Hrafntinnusker is highly symmetrical and is a little over 0.5 km^3 in volume. It is a modest-sized dome, but still significantly larger than some of the smaller plugs you saw around Brennisteinsalda.

Day Hikes

From Hrafntinnusker, there are several nice excursions you can make if you are motivated to walk further after the trek in from Landmannalaugar.

1. Íshellir (1-2 hrs)

   Just north of the hut, there is a trail junction where a short trail loops around the northern edge of the *obsidian* dome and leads to where, in previous years, a massive ice cave, Íshellir, had been. In 2008, the main cave collapsed. Smaller caves form and vanish all over the highlands each year. If you do come across a significant cave, count yourself lucky, but don't assume your luck will follow you inside the ice cave. Ice caves are notoriously unstable. In 2006, a man was killed by falling ice at Íshellir. Any cave can be dangerous, especially in the summer when melting is at a peak.

2. Söðull (40 min)

   A second day hike option climbs north and east from the campground to the summit of nearby Söðull. The climb is short and gentle (20 minutes) and leads to a fantastic 360° panorama of the surrounding terrain. The summit is covered by an amalgamation of massive and flow-banded *rhyolite* while the flanks are covered in pumice. Söðull is an excellent place to see the

Flow-banded rhyolite near the summit of Söðull

progressive change in eruptive behavior that many volcanoes experience.

Often, the first stage of an eruption will be an explosive phase. The *magma* initiating the eruption is gas-rich and full of volatiles. Söðull started out as an explosive fissure, spitting out ash, cinders and the blocks of pumice visible on the flanks. These are all considered *pyroclastic* products. As the *magma* degassed and the energy of the eruption waned, the character of the eruption switched from explosive to *effusive*. In this phase, high-viscosity lava was squeezed to the surface, much like toothpaste. Eventually, the lava cooled to the point that it was no longer mobile and the vent became plugged, ending the eruption. The *rhyolite* lava at the top of Söðull - was the plug that capped the eruptive vent. You can see beautiful iron staining and flow banding within the summit *rhyolite*.

3. Reykjafjöll

From Söðull, you can drop down the southeastern flank, cross a drainage, and scale the prominent peak of the Reykjafjöll (Smoke Mountains). This adds another hour or so to your hike, but from the summit you have an excellent view of Torfajökull and cluster of valleys draining to the east. There is a steep cliff between Reykjafjöll and the camping area. I recommend ascending and descending over near Söðull. However you go, walk carefully and tread lightly as there are no developed trails. Avoid walking on the moss, if possible.

Hrafntinnusker is usually the coldest night you will spend on the Laugavegur trail due to its high elevation and exposure to wind. If the temperature drops below 0° C, I like to boil up a liter of water and tuck a hot Nalgene into my sleeping bag with me. It will get you through the night even if you haul around an old and ratty sleeping bag. I have been advised that chocolate helps a bit too.

Day 2. Hrafntinnusker – Álftavatn
(12 km; 4 - 5 hours; Elevation decrease 490m)

Day 2 will hopefully begin with sun and clear skies, like the one pictured above, but if not, pull down your cap, button up your shell, and head due south toward Háskerðingur (1281m). The trail is again marked by tall yellow posts that stand out in all but complete white-out conditions (yes, I have experienced those hiking this section of the trail). Reykjafjöll will be on your left as you cruise through gently eroded valleys and flatlands. Depending on the time of year you pass through, some drainages will have snow bridges in various stages of decay. Use your best judgment on where to cross and do not automatically follow the footprints of others. Some paths that were reasonable the day before may have become unstable overnight.

Háskerðingur is the mountain upon which the smaller glacier, Kaldaklofsjökull rests. It is usually difficult to visually distinguish Kaldaklofsjökull from seasonal snowpack, at least when compared to the glacial behemoth Mýrdalsjökull, which becomes visible in the distance. As you approach Háskerðingur, the snow fields give way to the soft *rhyolite* hills again, and you climb up onto the southern rim of the Torfajökull *caldera*. There is a spur trail up Háskerðingur that provides yet another opportunity to take in a spectacular panorama.

Hiking to Háskerðingur

Cresting the rim of the *caldera*, you will notice a number of changes: 1) you switch over from colorful *rhyolite* to darker rock with abundant *palagonite*; 2) green groundcover becomes more abundant; and 3) visibility often improves as the *caldera* concentrates fog and cloud cover and the valley below is sometimes bathed in sunlight. No guarantees, but on top of that rim, just above Jökultungur, you have the chance to gaze for the first time on the verdant Álftavatn valley.

Off in the distance, Álftavatn lake (which is repetitively redundant because Álftavatn means Swan Lake - so Swan Lake lake) shimmers an icy teal, surrounded by steep green, black, and gray peaks. Mýrdalsjökull dominates the horizon left of the valley and Eyjafjallajökull rises directly behind Álftavatn. To the right of the valley is the smaller, but very rugged-looking Tindfjallajökull. Tindfjallajökull is composed of both *basalt* and *rhyolite*. A major *caldera* eruption that occurred about 54,000 years ago produced the Þórsmörk *pyroclastics*, which underlie many of the volcanic deposits we see today. This is my favorite panorama on the hike and I have been known to fill entire SD cards with photos trying, in vain, to capture the feeling.

Peaks surrounding the Álftavatn valley

From this vista, you can trace the remainder of the day's hike down to the southern shoreline of Álftavatn where the hut and a few colorful tents may be visible. Though it looks close enough from here, you are still about two hours out, so don't mentally pack it in for the day yet.

The Álftavatn valley is a rift valley. This means that the crust is being pulled apart here and that there are faults on either side of the lake. As the crust is pulled apart the faults allow for the center of the valley to subside, dropping down in elevation and creating areas for water and sediments to collect. The faults also act as conduits for *magma* bodies that are making their way to the surface. *Magma*, like water, will take the path of least resistance and pre-fractured rock is much easier to migrate through than solid bedrock. Consequently, volcanoes are very common along regional fault lines. In the picture below, you can see the Álftavatn rift valley and parallel valleys to the west that were created by the same extensional regional stress. Volcanic

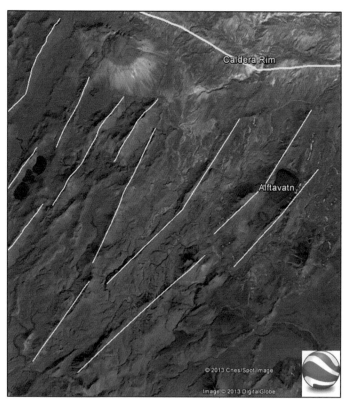

Sub-parallel rift valleys in the Álftavatn area.
Volcanic ridges marked in white

ridgelines mark the edges of each valley.

The trail down Jökultungur can get steep and is littered with rounded pebbles that can cause a level of anxiety. Take your time, watch your step, and eventually you will find yourselves along the banks of the modest river Grashagakvísl. In the spring or after a heavy rain, the water can be high, but usually, this river does not require wading. Depending on the flow and your leaping abilities, you can often rock/gravel-bar hop across. A few times I have found boards stretched across the river a little downstream of the main crossing area. Once across, it is a simple walk, skirting the northern edge of Torfatindar into the open valley bottom.

View across Álftavatn. Bratthals on the left.

Álftavatn

Looking out on this beautiful valley are two huts that house about 60 people in total. I highly recommend the camping, however. The average temperature is significantly warmer than Hrafntinnusker and the winds, much gentler. There is a large area for camping, allowing folks to spread out a bit, but please mind the signs asking you not to camp too close to the lake itself. The ground is very soft and the mosses are highly susceptible to

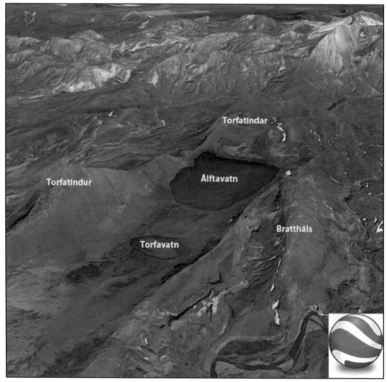

Overview of the primary features around Álftavatn

compaction. The valley is accessible by 4WD vehicle and occasionally you will see one come up one of the dirt paths. As of 2013, Reykjavik Excursions was offering bus service to Álftavatn. It comes through around midday so most hikers do not see the bus, but it is available.

Day Hikes

Most folks like to get out of Hrafntinnusker early in the morning and consequently find themselves in Álftavatn by early to mid-afternoon. This offers you the opportunity to explore the beautiful terrain around the lake in greater detail. Even if you arrive after dinner, you will likely still have hours of daylight left to explore unless you visit in very late summer.

1. Álftavatn Loop (1-2 hrs)

   For those wishing to avoid any additional climbing, there is a pleasant loop around Álftavatn. On the north side of the lake, there is a dirt track to follow and on the south side there is a small foot path. Beyond the far end of Álftavatn is Torfavatn, a smaller lake / bog area. The loop takes better than an hour to walk and there are many mental diversions and photo opportunities that can make it take even longer.

2. Bratthals (2hrs)

   Leaving the campsite you will have to cross a small creek and walk southeast toward the shoulder of Bratthals. You can scramble up the volcano's northeastern ridge. The elongate ridge-shaped morphology of Bratthals suggests that it was a fissure eruption along one of the regional faults mentioned earlier. As you climb, you will pass through several different types of deposits. First, you will see abundant *hyaloclastite* deposits that are indicative of *magma*-water interactions. As the lava reached the Earth's surface it came into contact with significant amounts of

Hyaloclastite deposit on northern flank of Bratthals

water or ice. In this case, ice or snowpack seems most likely. As the ice and snow flashed to steam, they caused violent explosions that inefficiently fractured the lava into particles ranging from ash to cobble in size. The entire deposit was subsequently welded.

You will then pass through *palagonite* deposits, like those you saw on the descent down Jökultungur. These deposits are laminar in many places, but elsewhere they can look quite turbulent. These deposits were produced by *pyroclastic surges. Surges* are produced when the *magma:* water ratios are relatively high. The explosions

Pyroclastic surge deposits up near summit vent

become more efficient, pulverizing the lava into particles, ranging from ash to pebble-sized. At the very summit, you see spires and squeeze-ups of coherent *lava.* You can literally see where the *lava* plugs were deformed as they were forced up through narrow vents.

Bratthâls tells a perfectly sequential story based on the deposits along the walk to the summit. The volcano must have been initiated along the fissure when the area was covered by glacial ice, thus the lower portion of the volcano has abundant *hyaloclastite* deposits. As the eruption progressed, the overlying ice was slowly melted away. Lava continued to erupt, but now instead of being inundated with ice, it encountered only melt water from the glacial ice surrounding the vent. This led to the production of the more efficient and explosive *pyroclastic surges*. Finally, the volcano grew to a point that the rising lava was extruded above all remaining ice and melt water. Thus, it did not explode and was forced out in the squeeze-ups that are visible right near the summit.

You can actually tell roughly how thick the ice sheet was by measuring the difference in elevation between the valley bottom and the point at which the coherent lava begins. Based on my measurements we are looking at an ice sheet that was only 200-225m thick when Bratthals was erupted. As a Bratthals side-trip scavenger hunt, see if you can find the squirrel-shaped spire pictured below:

There must be some Icelandic myth regarding a giant squirrel turning into stone, but I have not the reference.

3. Torfatindar and Torfatindur

The Álftavatn valley is bounded to the northwest by the sister ridges Torfatindar and Torfatindur. These two peaks are the result of sub-glacial fissure eruptions, just like Bratthals. They are likely of about the same age as well. I have not climbed the southern volcano, Torfatindur; it looks a bit gnarly, but I have walked the entire spine of the friendlier, yet surprisingly slick Torfatindar. I use the term slick, because like Jökultungur, there are areas where hard, welded ash beds are covered with loose, rounded pebbles that could make for a nasty slide if you misstep. Much of the hike across the ridge is quite pleasant, and this volcano also tells a story.

View of Torfatindar from the summit of Bratthals

Access to Torfatindar is best at Álftaskard, the road-cut gap at the southern end of the volcano. Here you can scale your way up to the ridge. Looking west, you can see the soft sodded plains of Torfamýrar (*Torfi's Marshes*). As you climb, you will pass thick deposits of *hyaloclastites*, similar to those seen on Bratthals and Jökultungur. Just at the ridge top you will see a different type of deposit called *pillow lava*. In this case, *pillow basalt* has been formed. These types of deposits form when small volumes of lava are injected into deep, standing water. The section of Torfatindar that produced the *pillow basalt* is significantly lower in elevation than

Pillow lava formations outlined in white

Bratthals. Between the presence of pillows and the lower overall elevation, geologists surmise that unlike Bratthals, Torfatindar never completely breeched the overlying glacier. The vent was perpetually inundated with ice and melt water providing the confining pressure to prevent explosions and produce the pillows.

It appears that Torfatindar was the product of at least two separate eruptive events. The southwestern reach of the ridge is softly rounded and covered by *hyaloclastite* and the *pillow lava* deposits described above. This was the part of the fissure that did not pierce the overlying glacier.

Just north of the rounded section, you can see the jagged ridge line of a second eruptive phase. It is difficult to tell just by shape whether the jagged ridge predates, postdates or was coeval with the rounded section. What can be determined is that the northern part of Torfatindar did melt through the overlying glacier. As you walk along the spine, you can see coherent lava squeeze-ups that suggest the lava was minimally affected by water interactions. There are also two major vent craters and several minor

Lava squeeze-up

craters on the very northeastern end of Torfatindar suggesting that, for a time, the eruption was sub-aerial. Once you have taken it all in, enjoy the scramble back down to camp.

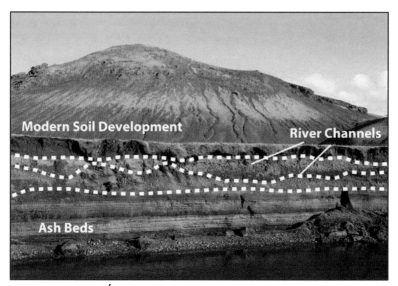

Álftavatn campground outcrop

Directly across the stream that circles around the Álftavatn camping area is an excellent exposure. Here, you can see the accumulated layers of ash and lake mud, overlain by stream deposits. The ash/mud layers are relatively thin and laminar. The ash deposits are likely from the last 10,000 years and have been erupted by a myriad of different volcanic centers, including Hekla, Katla, Torfajökull; maybe even a dusting from Laki, Vatnaöldur, or Grimsvötn.

Ripples within volcanic ash deposits indicating wind or water reworking between eruptive events

Day 3. Álftavatn – Emstrur-Botnar
(15 km; 6-7 hours; Elevation decrease 40m)

Time to hit the trail again! As you leave the green oasis of Álftavatn, you will barely have time to clip your pack before you reach a tributary leading to Bratthálskvisl. It is all of a foot deep, quietly meandering its way to Álftavatn. I've seen many hikers splash their way through the stream in their boots, but they usually get wetter than they anticipate. I'm not saying it can't be done, but I usually error on taking off my boots and fording the gentle stream as opposed to starting the day off with sopping feet.

A Note on River Crossings:

Though Bratthálskvisl may seem gentle, the rivers you will cross today and tomorrow are no joke. They are cold, quick, and full of rounded, mobile cobbles. One year, I tried to save weight and did not bring a pair of "river shoes". I forded the rivers bare-foot and regretted it. Slipping, I split my toenail and limped the last 30k. Bring a pair of shoes; closed toe are the best, but bring at least hearty strap-on sandals. You will be able to move more quickly and securely. The weight is well worth it. When crossing fast moving or deep water, unbuckle your pack so you can slip out of it easily should you fall. Link arms with others in your group and angle yourselves slightly upstream. Move across the river together, using one another for support.

Starting out Day 3

Past the tributary the trail climbs up and over the shoulder of Brattháls before dropping down toward the snub-peaked mountains Ófæra and Ófæruhöfði. Here you cross Bratthálskvisl proper. Usually, this is a fairly gentle crossing with a large gravel bar in the middle to shake your feet out a bit. The water is COLD and you will feel discomfort by the time you exit the far side. Your feet hurt, but man, you feel alive!

Across Bratthálskvisl, you enter Hvanngil, the *"Angelic Valley"*, which is, perhaps, an understatement. Green and black peaks rise up all around, pouring out small streams of cold, clear water. The wildflowers here are fantastic and often you have the feeling that faeries play in and around the mossy mounds. On sunny days, you have to remind yourself to keep moving as you still have many kilometers to cover before you sleep. To your right is the unreasonably photogenic volcano, Stórasúla.

I have a mistress… and her name is Stórasúla

Skirting around the corner of Ófæra you come upon a small settlement with two huts and several other buildings. One hut was built for sheepherders in 1963 and the other was built specifically for tourists in 1995. You are able to camp here and some folks choose Hvannagil's vistas over Álftavatn's or decide to migrate further if Álftavatn looks crowded. Hvannagil offers a side-hike along a dirt track up into Mælifellssandur; an area of seemingly endless *basalt* flats. You can make your way over to the base of Mýrdalsjökull along this route, but it is a full day's detour.

At the trail junction just past the huts, you have the shorter day-hike option of summiting either Hvanngilshausar by turning east at the junction or Hvanngilskrókur by turning west. Either way will lead you to a beautiful overlook of the entire valley.

Overlooking the Hvannagil valley

The trail snakes around the settlement and ultimately takes you through a well-formed lava flow. Within the flow you can see collapsed lava tubes, push-up ridges, and small spatter vents called *hornitos*. This lava is *basalt* and though it is similar in color to the *obsidian* flows you saw on day one, its chemistry is very different. *Obsidian* is very *felsic* (high silica content), while *basalt* is very *mafic* (low silica content). From here on out, *basalt* will be the primary flavor of lava.

Leaving the lava flow, you will reach the river, Kaldaklofskvísl, where a bridge has been constructed. Dry feet! Joy! But the joy is short-lived as you are plunged into Bláfjallakvisl less than a kilometer later. You will be glad to have your river shoes for this crossing. It is only knee-deep, but it is wide and short-breathed cussing is the norm.

View of Kaldaklofskvísl from the bridge.

Dry your feet well and lace up your boots because you are headed into the *basalt* desert. Grains of sand that get around your heels or toes will irritate you to blisters over the next few kilometers, if you are not careful. You start out along the 4WD track as Stórasúla and Súluhryggir pass to the northwest and Smáfjallarani, Smáfjöll, and finally, Stórkonufell pass to the southeast. All the while, Mýrdalsjökull grows larger and larger on the horizon. At Innri-Emstruá, you will be pleased to be provided a bridge to help you across a rather mighty river with an impressive set of falls just downstream of the bridge. The far side is a decent lunch spot, though you will have company during peak season.

Stórkonufell: You know it's true.

Continue southwest toward the low hill Útigönguhöfðar. Just before reaching Útigönguhöfðar, the trail breaks to the south and the 4WD track continues up north of the next prominent cone, Hattfell. Coming across the low pass over Útigönguhöfðar you turn right, toward the base of Hattfell.

Cloud shadows play on the slopes of Hattfell

You will pass another small stream crossing before you enter an area that is absolutely littered with *bombs*. Do not be alarmed, these *bombs* are not explosive, but are rather volcanic, meaning that they formed when gobs of molten lava were shot out of a vent. As the gobs flew on their ballistic path, they cooled somewhat before slamming into the ground. The relative amount of cooling prior to impact is reflected in the shape and texture of the *bomb* itself. The *bombs* along this stretch came from the two recent cones, Tuddi and Tvíbaka. In another geological scavenger hunt, see if you can find the four *bomb* types listed here;

- Spherical *bombs* form when the lava is very low viscosity and surface tension is able to keep the *magma* spherical in shape.
- Cored *bombs* form when existing rock fragments are covered in molten material before being launched out of the vent. There is a distinct margin where the hot *magma* contacts the relatively "cool" existing rock fragment. These fragments could be pieces of bedrock or chunks of rock from an earlier eruption.
- Bread crust *bombs* are created when the outer skin of a lava *bomb* cools while flying through the air. The inside remains molten and continues to degas and expand, creating the flaky crust-like texture.
- Finally, cow pie *bombs* are the result of molten lava that impacts the ground while still mostly fluid. It is a visual analogy, you see.

Spherical Bomb   **Cored Bomb**

Bread Crust Bomb   **Cowpie Bomb**

Shortly after your journey through the land of volcanic *bombs*, you will drop down onto the Markarfljót plateau from which you can see your stop for the night, Botnar.

Emstrur-Botnar

There are several buildings at the Botnar camp; cabins for up to 40 people, a warden's hut, and a separate bathroom facility. The campsite at Botnar is

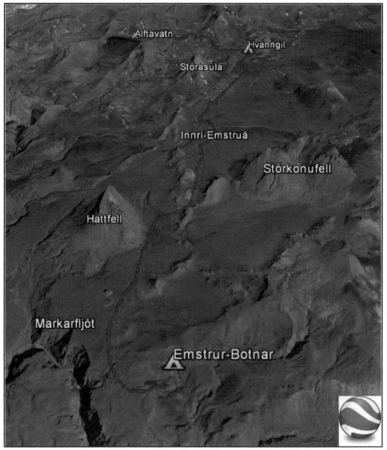

Day three trek; Álftavatn to Botnar.

probably the tightest-packed campground on the Laugavegur trail. Flat ground is at a premium and during peak season, tents will be right on top of each other. Ear plugs my friends, ear plugs. There are additional campsites along the drainage to the right of the main camping area. They are around a corner so most folks do not see them. If there is a spot to have a little more space, it is there. The skyline is dominated by Mýrdalsjökull and one can finally begin to appreciate the climbing that will be required to get to the pass between Mýrdalsjökull and Eyjafjallajökull in two days' time.

Trail junction to take you to Markarfljótgljúfur

Day Hikes

1. <u>Markarfljótgljúfur Canyon (1-2 hrs)</u>

   The best way to spend an evening at Botnar is to climb up and explore Markarfljótgljúfur. The trail for the canyon overlook splits off of the main trail just above Botnar. You will likely have seen the sign when you first descended into camp. The trail is marked with small wooden posts that lead to several vantage points from which you can peer over cliff edges into the steep and rugged canyon. Every river you crossed since coming down from Hrafntinnusker eventually feeds into the Markarfljót. From here it braids out over the glacial outwash plains from Mýrdalsjökull and Eyjafjallajökull and 25 kilometers distant, it finally pours into the north Atlantic.

   The views from above the canyon are astounding as the torrential waters have efficiently sliced through over 200m of lava flows and *pyroclastic* deposits. Vent areas from preexisting volcanoes show up rusty red on the canyon wall facing you. You can trace individual lava flows for hundreds of meters. Again, it is important to exercise caution when exploring the canyon's edge. Often we are lulled into a false sense of security, but erosion happens. Trails and overlooks crumble as easily as any rock along the edge of the canyon.

**Dwarf alpine willow
(Salix herbacea)**

At the very southwestern edge of the plateau, you can see tall waterfalls where tributaries add their two pennies to the powerful flow below. In late July and Early August, the Markarfljót plateau is covered with arctic beauties and dwarf alpine willow. You can wander the plateau for quite a while. Looking northwest you see the canyon cut. Looking southwest you see the canyon snake out toward the ocean, disappearing into a vast complex of hills and drainages that you will be able to explore tomorrow. Looking south you can see where the trail climbs through the pass at Fimmvörðuháls. Once you have gotten your fill of panoramas, head back to camp and sleep hard. Tomorrow, we head to Thor's Realm!

**Arctic river beauty
(Chamerion latifolium)**

Day 4. Emstrur-Botnar - Þórsmörk

(15 km; 6-7 hrs; Elevation decrease 300m)

Today's hike will take you across a thunderous canyon before you turn south and skirt the Markarfljót canyon all the way down to Þórsmörk. The hike is relatively gentle and most rivers are crossed by way of bridges.

Day 4 begins by heading out from the campground area. You are immediately greeted by a sign that discusses danger areas and evacuation procedures should Katla get restless. Many tourists from countries not living in the shadow of a volcano may look at this sign light-heartedly, but I assure you, the signs are there for good reason. You are crossing over into valleys and drainages that would be flooded or otherwise cut-off by *jökulhlaups* released from Mýrdalsjökull if Katla they were to have even the most modest of eruptions.

Markarfljót Canyon

In 2011, a *jökulhlaup* was initiated from a very minor eruption on Katla. Though the eruption was small, the *jökulhlaup* was large enough to take out a large roadway bridge on the ring road, Route 1. How big can these *jökulhlaups* get? In 1918, *jökulhlaups* from a Katla eruption extended the coastline of Iceland by 3km. Yeah, big.

Evacuation protocol sign outside Botnar

My Poorly Translated Saga of Katla

Many years ago, not long after Christianity spread to Iceland, there was a monastery nestled in among the verdant hills at the base of Mýrdalsjökull. It was a, by all measure, a successful monastery, tending to the souls of the nearby villages while producing some fantastic wine. Grapes in Iceland? Sure, why not? The monastery was headed by a kind and gentle Abbot who oversaw the daily operations. Also working at the monastery was a dark and sinister woman named Katla. She had a horrific temper and no insult, real or completely imagined, was too small to set her off. Many of the villagers believed her to be a witch, but of course, nobody would come out and accuse her and all stayed out of her way as best they could. Even the Abbott wilted before her.

It is told that Katla had a pair of magical britches. Now, I'm a little fuzzy on the translation here as to whether britches mean pants or underwear; whatever visual works for you. Either way, the magical britches would allow anyone who wore them to run as fast as the wind and never tire. Why these were particularly useful to a cleaning woman, I am not sure.

One villager, Barði, was in charge of keeping track of the monastery's sheep. One evening he came back from the pastures to see Katla standing by the back gate. She was furious, saying that he had been neglecting his duties and that a sheep was missing. Barði went and counted the sheep and to his horror he realized Katla was right and they were one sheep short. Katla threatened to curse him if he did not get the sheep back. Barði grabbed a lantern and headed out into the night. For hours he searched to no avail. He just could not cover enough ground. If only he had some way of moving about more quickly... a horse, or maybe... some magic britches?!?!

Barði ran back to the monastery and snuck in through the back door. Down the hallway, he could hear Katla yelling at some poor servant. He crept into Katla's room and rummaged around in her trunk until he found an elegant, lacy, pair of britches. Hillocks and valleys passed beneath his feet one after another, yet he never tired. Shortly, he was able to find the wayward sheep and he quickly returned to the monastery. Putting the lost sheep up, he stole his way back into Katla's room and replaced the britches.

The next day, Barði was working in the winery mashing up grapes when Katla thundered through the door. She had fire in her eyes. *She knew.* Maybe he had folded them wrong or something, but Katla knew he had been wearing her britches. In a rage, Katla suffocated Barði in the grape pulp and threw his body into the wine vat. Knowing that in time the body would be discovered, Katla grabbed her britches and ran up atop Mýrdalsjökull and lowered herself into a deep crevasse. Not long after, the Abbott found Barði's body and organized the villagers to go after Katla. They were making their way up the Krossá river valley when a huge explosion came from Mýrdalsjökull. A wall of water descended from the melting glacier and swept away many of the party. It was Katla's warning. Come no closer. Since that day, the volcano and all its ill-tempered activities have been attributed to the great witch Katla and her magic britches.

The signs show where *Jökulhlaups* have flowed in the past and the best escape routes should an eruption occur. In such a scenario, the huts have flares and cannon-like firecrackers to warn trekkers to move to high ground. The area is on special alert right now due to increased seismicity around Katla and the fact that Eyjafjallajökull had a significant eruption in 2010. In the last 1000 years, Eyjafjallajökull has erupted three times and each time the eruption was followed shortly by a significant eruption from Katla. This suggests that there may be some connection in the *magma* plumbing that feeds both volcanic systems. Volcanologists continue to monitor Katla and Eyjafjallajökull, both of which seem to be settled in an uneasy period of quiescence.

Bridges over Syðri-Emstruá

Past the sign, you will loop around to the exciting river crossing at Syðri – Emstruá. A sandy path that uses ropes to aid in the descent leads down to two well-constructed bridges across a narrow canyon. Staring straight down provides an interesting perspective on the down-cutting activities of the river. Climbing out the other side, you emerge onto another sand flat. To the east, a large sand flat leads back to Entujökull, or the "Enduring Glacier". The cliff at the edge of the sand flat shows an excellent exposure of *columnar basal. Columnar basalt* forms as thick lava flows of *basalt* cool in place. During the cooling process, the *basalt* contracts and forms hexagonal columns. Six-sided columns are the most common, though columns with 3-12 sides have been reported. Generally, the quicker the rate of cooling, the smaller the column's diameter. Sometimes columns radiate out from a central point. This was an area of sustained heat; often, the heart of the lava flow. Both radiating and vertical columnar *basalt* outcrops are visible along this stretch of the trail.

Radial columnar basalt

Continuing down the trail, ridges stack upon one another to the east while the Markarfljót is your constant companion to the west. Rising on the horizon to the west is the sinister looking, horned peak, Einhyrningur. The name pleasantly translates to "unicorn" though I know it is, in fact, dragon's aerie. The diligent observer will potentially* see two or three dragons circling the peak. So, you know, keep an eye out. You can apparently summit Einhyrningur from the 4WD track that splits off the Laugavegur trail around Hattfell. I have not climbed it yet, but I have heard dragon-egg omelets are delicious, so perhaps next year.

Continuing south, barren *basalt* flows and sand flats give way to more lush vegetation. Shrubs

Photo by: Scott Marshall

Unicorn Mountain... I mean Fire-breathing Death Unicorn Mountain

* Probability of dragon sighting, just shy of .00000000001%

54

and grasses get thicker and taller as you descend toward the Þórsmörk valley. A bridge will take you across the narrow canyon that confines the Ljósá River. Shortly after, you will climb a significant ridge marking the Þórsmörk boundary. From the ridgetop, you can look down on the final river to be forded, the Þrönga. Þrönga means "narrow" and the irony of the name for the widest river on the trail is not lost here.

The Þrönga is a braided, gravel-rich river that can be crossed by fording from one gravel bar to the next. Usually there are 3-4 channels that you must negotiate. Pick your spots carefully as some areas are surprisingly deep or quick. By this point you are a fording veteran and the river should not cause too much stress. Braided rivers are common glacial outwash plains as the channels are choked with abundant sediments, leading to multiple, migratory channels.

Immediately on the other side of the river, you enter Þórsmörk; Thors's woods. Feel free to yell "mörk" in celebration of seeing your first trees all trip. I always do, even though the translation isn't really correct. You will be surrounded by stunted birch, aspen, and rowan trees and it will feel new, different, and lovely.

The narrow, Þrönga River

Photo by: Scott Marshall

Þórsmörk

A trail junction, not too far ahead, allows you to decide your fate for the evening. There are three separate campsites around Þórsmörk; Húsadalur, Langidalur, and Básar. Húsadalur is the closest camp with the most amenities. I've visited a few times and have sampled the ice cream, but not the hot pool. I know myself and once I enter a hot pool, I will not want to get up and hike more. If you arrive at any camp around midday, you should be able to catch a Reykjavik Excursions bus back to Reykjavik, if you so choose. In recent years, the busses have been stopping at each camp between 1 and 3:30PM, but check the bus schedule before you go as schedules are prone to alteration and seasonal changes.

Sign showing variety of diversions near Þórsmörk

The swankiest accommodations are found at the Volcano Huts, a short way west of the Húsadalur campground. I have never had the honor, but word on the street is that in addition to having a well-stocked bar and grille, they also provide yoga classes, massage, and the thermal delights of a sauna and hot pool. I can sure think of worse ways of ending a 4-day excursion. It can be expected that with increased tourist traffic in Iceland, the commercial offerings at Þórsmörk will continue to diversify.

If you, like me, want to complete the entire journey over Fimmvörðuháls to Skógar, you will want to head toward Langidalur and then ultimately, Básar. Langidalur is probably the least crowded of the Þórsmörk campsites. It has water and restrooms, but the "café" has not been open the last few times I have hiked past. Definitely do not count on it for resupply. A bus with service back to Reykjavik stops here to pick up passengers in the early afternoon. Leaving Langidalur, the trail dumps you out into the Krossá River valley. The trail just disappears. If you follow the vehicle tracks, you will come to a place that big busses and burly 4WD SUV's can cross the river.

DO NOT TRY TO CROSS HERE! People have died trying to ford the river at this location. My first time approaching the Krossá, I strode confidently toward it and started taking off my shoes before my hiking companion grabbed me, shook me, and said, "Bad Idea!" He more sang it actually, like an operatic baritone. We tossed a few rocks in and they didn't make that splashing sound of shallow water, but rather that deep thunk of water over a meter in depth. This thing (below) drove by and the water was at the top of the tires.

Bad idea, indeed!

The best and safest way to cross the Krossá on foot is to hike upstream (toward Básar) about a kilometer where two mobile bridges have been rolled across the river. The bridges have to remain mobile so they can adjust to the changing channels of the braided river. In future years the bridges may be moved, but whatever the situation, do not attempt to cross the Krossá by fording it. Many people hike across the river each day; there will always be a safe way to get across. Ask a warden or fellow hiker or hitch a ride on a huge bus, just please, do not try to cross it on foot.

As of 2013, the bridges looked like this...

An interesting aspect of the Þórsmörk valley is that, since the Eyjafjallajökull eruption in 2010, the area has been subject to inundation by ash whenever a breeze kicks up on the Fimmvörðuháls pass. It appears as a thick fog. You can taste it. Wardens in the area keep tabs on the strength

The ash, while destroying the panoramas, adds a completely different type of dynamic beauty to Þórsmörk

and direction of the wind and they can tell you how pleasant your hike over the Fimmvörðuháls pass will likely be. One year, we caught a significant wind and the Krossá river valley reminded me of my home near the Smoky Mountains.

Once across the bridges, it is a short walk to the Básar campground. Like Langidalur, there is no reliable food service at this campground, though there are grills for grilling. Básar is popular with weekend campers in Iceland and you will see some intricate tent palaces erected as Icelanders celebrate the long days of summer. A side effect is, of course, that the camp

Natural rock bridge near Þórsmörk

can get crowded and loud occasionally. Luckily, there are many secluded campsites to the east of the main campground that are much quieter. The only downside is that you have a long hike for fresh water and the bathroom. On the plus side, you are closer to the Fimmvörðuháls trailhead.

Photo by: Scott Marshall

Looking down on Básar from nearby Fálkhöfuð

Day Hikes

The day hikes around Þórsmörk are even more numerous than those at Landmannalaugar. It would be a guidebook in of itself describing all the options available and it would be a guide that I would be ill-qualified to write as I have only explored a few of the side trails and valleys. But, I will share a few hikes I have explored on some level and encourage you to explore more. Hiking maps for Þórsmörk are available for purchase in Reykjavik and at the Volcano Huts. The Serkort #4 map, mentioned several times in this guide has a detailed map of Þórsmörk (1:50,000) on the back side of the main map. This is detail enough to get you to the trailheads and to plan out basic routes, though the resolution is still too low to get any but the most basic idea of the trail contours.

Þórsmörk is well signed but there is a dog's breakfast of trails in the vicinity that can be disorienting to first-time visitors. Make use of the signs and your map.

1. Valahnúker (1 hr)
   A short climb from either Húsadalur or Langidalur will take you to the peak, Valahnúker. Some of the best views in Þórsmörk can be seen from this readily accessible peak. An hour's worth of hiking for some spectacular views? Yes, Please! Low hanging fruit, my friends. Take advantage.

2. Stakkholtsgjá (4 hrs)
   This is a longer hike from Básar that takes you through the Hvannárgil valley to a beautiful waterfall tucked up in the Stakkholtsgjá gorge. The out and back trip takes around 2hrs in each direction. The year I hiked it, there was one bridge over the Hvanná River but several streams had to be rock-hopped. During periods of high flow, wading might be necessary.

Day 5. Þórsmörk – Skógar

(25 km; 10-12 hrs; Elevation decrease 100m overall, but you have to climb around 900m up to the Fimmvörðuháls pass).

Eat a hearty breakfast, slather on some chapstick, and strap your pack on tight. You are into it now. Today, you will climb up over the Fimmvörðuháls pass and on to Skógar. It is a long day, starting with a 900m ascent. Though it is a sustained and at times, grueling climb, the trail twists and skirts through truly magical lands.

Leaving Básar, you will continue east along the marked trail (It has been different colors in different years, but it is always well signed). A bridge will take you across a tributary to the Krossá before making a sharp right up into the hills surrounding the Strákagil valley. As you skirt the first ridge, named Fálkhöfuð, the morning sun will be rising just in front of you, casting dynamic light across the valley. The trees quickly fade behind you as you climb up toward mossy plains covered in low shrubs and wildflowers. You will likely recognize many plants from earlier in the trip.

Útigönguhöfði rising up in the middle of Goðaland

Manufactured steps help you along to the next ridge, Kattahryggur (*Sad Cat*). There must be a story behind the name. I don't know it, so make one up. To your right is the prominent peak, named Útigönguhöfði. It is at the heart of what is known as the Abode Of The Gods or Goðaland. This area includes the Hvanná River mentioned in the day hikes as well as Strákagil valley, which you can see to your right. The trail narrows to a knife edge in some areas, providing great views to the left and right. At one spot a rope has been installed to help you scale a particularly weathered section. Climb this rope one at a time. If a second person hops on the rope at the bottom, while the first is near the top, the first person can be pulled off a cliff. Don't ask…

Thanks. The trail loops around before the Heiðarhorn blocks your way with a wall 200m tall. There is no option but to put your head down for the steepest sustained climb you will have on the entire journey. The top is the Morinsheiði plateau. From this vantage point you can finally catch a view of the summit *caldera* on Eyjafjallajökull. Directly ahead of you on the trail are the massive lava falls from the 2010 eruption. They are stark black against the surrounding grey and as of 2013, they were still steaming.

Lava Falls from 2010 Eyjafjallajökull eruption

The lava flowed from the highland off a cliff into the Hrunagil valley where it mixed with glacial melt water. You will see much more from this lava flow once you are on top of the pass.

In order to get there, you have to negotiate another rope / wire assisted traverse. This crossing is located at the base of Heljarkambur point which uncomfortably translates to something about graves and climbing. Make sure nobody is on the descent before committing to the traverse as passing on the traverse requires master-level dexterity and balance. Topping out Heljarkambur puts all the serious climbing behind you. You can now enjoy the fruits of your labor, which include a walk alongside the massive 2010 lava flow and your first peek at the two summit cones produced during the eruption, Móði and Magni.

Eyjafjallajökull Eruption 2010

The story of the Eyjafjallajökull eruption began in 2009 when seismicity increased beneath the glacier indicating that *magma* was on the move. Geological monitoring of the volcano was increased. By the time the fissure opened up on March 20th of 2010, officials were well-prepared and a strategic plan was put into motion. People in danger zones were quickly evacuated and roads susceptible to *jökulhlaups* were pre-emptively closed. For the rest of March and part of April small explosions occurred and lava poured from the fissure, eventually focusing down into the two vent cones seen today.

On April 14th, after a brief hiatus in activity, the eruption changed character and went explosive. The active vent shifted from the Fimmvörðuháls pass to beneath the Eyjafjallajökull glacier. Massive amounts of glacial melting initiated several *jökulhlaups* and threatened many homes. The Þórsmörk area was evacuated along with 700 people living along the Markarfljót drainage. Ash drifted to the south and east, blanketing farmland and shutting down air traffic over much of Europe. By May 23rd all eruptive activity had ceased and the volcano settled into an uneasy rest. Overall, the eruption was modest, with a *VEI* of 4. As mentioned earlier, Eyjafjallajökull eruptions in the last 1000 years have habitually been followed by major eruptions by Katla within a few months. Whether or not Katla will produce a major eruption in the next few years is still unknown.

The cones are named after Thor's sons; Móði (Angry) and Magni (Strong)

Both cones, Móði and Magni, can be easily scrambled to terrific 360⁰ views. Looking east, you see the extent to which the lava flowed during the *effusive* primary stage of the eruption and looking west, you can see the outline of the *caldera* on Eyjafjallajökull where the subsequent explosive phase of the eruption took place. The lava flows to the east comprise *basalt* chunks that are loose, sharp and irregular in shape. This type of flow texture is called A'a and results from slow-moving thick lobes of lava that cool as they move down slope. The cooled top and front margins of the flow break apart making the irregular chunks. A'a flows are very difficult and dangerous to walk on, even when cool. Step carefully. All around the cones and lava flows there are active and powerful *fumaroles*. Oxidation and alteration of the rocks in the vicinity of *fumaroles* have turned the black *basalt* various shades of pink and red. As of 2013, the ground was still warm to the touch in many places. This can be of great benefit if you want to stop for lunch, but don't want to get chilled.

Fimmvörðuháls

The Fimmvörðuháls pass is actually quite broad and the descent toward Skógar does not begin until you cross almost 2 kilometers of flatland. The pass is mottled with snow fields and ash. Some of the snow fields have interesting piles of cinders on them. These miniature mountain ranges are found on glaciers and snowfields all around Eyjafjallajökull. I am not certain of what the causes the pilings, but I hypothesize that they are the result of the cinders acting as insulation for the snow or ice beneath. As such, during

Cinder piles atop Fimmvörðuháls

warmer days, the snow beneath the piles is preserved while the barren snow continues to melt, exacerbating the difference in height between the two. On very sunny days, the process may reverse some as the black cinders warm in the direct sunlight. Fortunately, sunny days are not all that common and the cinder piles remain. At Hrafntinnusker, I saw an interesting honeycomb structure that may be the start or a derivative of this process.

At the southern edge of the pass you will find two huts. Higher up is the hut owned by Útivist, an Icelandic hiking group. The lower one, Baldvinsskáli is a bit more worn and not as well stocked. Over the first 4 days, water was not an issue due to the regular river crossings and relatively short total hiking distances. On the final day over Fimmvörðuháls, water can be an issue if you only carry a quart or two. On top of the plateau, you will find plenty of snow to melt, but there is no running water to speak of until you are well on your way down the descent. The huts' water is supplied exclusively by rain catchment and they are not able to replenish hikers' empty bottles. The water available from glacial runoff on the descent is fantastic, so hold out for it.

Glacial honeycomb texture from Hrafntinnusker

At the Útivist hut, you can stop in and see Ulie or one of the other caretakers if they are not busy. Ulie's story is perfect for a hut caretaker; he is retired, loves the outdoors, taking care of folks, and chatting up strangers. He directed us to the best water to refill our bottles on the descent and a few alternate, more visually stimulating ways of getting down off the pass. The main path sweeps past Baldvinsskáli and continues toward the eastern tributary of the Skóga River. One variation is marked with red wooden posts and parallels the western tributary. Eventually, the trails merge back together at a bridge over the Skóga, just north of the confluence of the two branches.

Here you will start to see numerous day-hikers on their way up from Skógar. Over the next 6-7 km you will pass a dozen waterfalls, any of which would be the crown jewel waterfall in most places. I call it the "Foss Festival". It is not a clever name, but you get kind of punchy by that point in the hike and you say stuff over and over till it sticks. The descent is gradual and entirely pleasant. Icelandic sheep give you nods of greeting from their perches on cliff sides. Slowly, Eyjafjallajökull falls away beyond the top of the pass. You will cross the Króksa River and another tributary as you pass the seemingly endless stretch of unique and beautiful waterfalls.

You are happy to see Skógar as the end of a long day approaches and you are welcomed to the campsite by one last giant, beautiful waterfall, Skógafoss. The thundering river drops 60m with a power and elegance that must be experienced to be understood.

Photo by: Scott Marshall

Skógar

Skógar is located just off the ring road and is easily accessible via the public bus system. There is both a campground and hostel at the base of the falls as well as a decent café. You will likely have to spend an evening in Skógar before catching a bus the next day unless you plow through the hike and arrive early in the afternoon. Whereas hitchhiking to Landmannalaugar is not really a dependable mode of conveyance, I have seen a few people catch rides from Skógar back to Reykjavik or Selfoss. The campground at Skógar is well-kept and there is a large lawn for the many campers to spread out on.

By this point, you will know many people in the camp, at least by sight, as you will have spent the last five days hiking and camping alongside them. Say hello and congratulate them for you are now part of a small world-wide fraternity of stout souls who have hiked the Laugavegur Trail.

Poor Translations:

Álftavatn – Swan lake

Baldvinsskáli – Bald popular lodge

Bláfjallakvisl – Blue mountain river confluence

Bláhnúkur - Blue peak

Botnar – Bottom land

Bratthály – Steep neck

Bratthálskvisl – Bratthály confluence

Brennisteinsalda – Sulfur Wave

Einhyrningur - Unicorn

Entugjá – Enduring gap

Entujökull – Enduring glacier

Eyjafjallajökull – Island mountain glacier

Fálkhöfuð – Falcon's head

Fimmvörðuháls – Five cairns pass

Foss - Falls

Gjá – Gap

Gljúfur - Canyon

Grænagil - Green gorge

Grashagakvísl – River of the meadow

Gráskalli - Gray bald

Grimsvötn – Stark waters

Háalda – high smooth mountain

Hattfell – Embedded, or "Hat cone"

Heiðarhorn – Horn of the sky

Heljarkambur – Grave cam

Hekla – Small, hooded cloak

Húsadalur – Valley house

Hvanngil – Angelic valley

Hvannárgil – Another angelic valley

Hvanngilshausar – Home of the Angels

Hvanngilskrókur – Angel's catch

Ilihryggur – Sorry party

Innrí-Emstruá – Inner Emstrur

Íshellir – Ice Cave

Jökulgil – Generic "Glacial Valley"

Jökultungur – Glacial tongue

Katla – Derivative of *kettil* meaning "Kettle"

Kattahryggur – Sad Cat

Kaldaklofsjökull – Cold, straddling glacier

Kaldaklofskvísl – Cold, straddling river confluence

Kvísl – Branch as in a river

Króksa – Shepherds hook

Krossá - Cross

Langidalur – Long Valley

Laugahraun – Bathing lava

Langháls – Long neck

Ljósártunger – Reflective tongue

Ljósá – Reflective River

Markarfljót - Mark of the River

Markarfljótgljúfur - Mark of the river canyon

Mælifellssandur – Sand of the Mountain

Mófell – Peat cone

Morinsheiði – Morin's heath

Mýrdalsjökull – Mire dale or Mire valley glacier

Námskvísl – Wise river

Norðurnámur – Northern quarry

Ófæra – Incapacitate

Ófæruhöfði – Debilitating point

Reykjafjöll – Smoke mountains

Rjúpnafell – Ptarmigan cone

Sandar - Sandy

Skarð – Pass

Söðull – Side-saddle

Smáfjallarani – Little mountain spur

Smáfjöll – Little mountain

Stakkholtsgjá – Stack hollow gap

Strákagil – The boys valley

Stóra-Grænafjall – Large green mountain

Stóra-Mófell – Large peat cone

Stórasúla – Large Column

Stórkonufell – Large woman cone (Big Mama?)

Suðurnámur – Southern Quarry

Súluhryggir – Columned ridges

Syðri-Emstruá – Southern Emstruá river

Þrönga – Narrow

Þórsmörk – Thor's woods or Thor's boarderland.

Tindfjallajökull – Peaked mountain Glacier

Torfajökull – Torfi's glacier after the historical figure Torfi Jónsson í Klofa (Torf also means Turf)

Torfamýrar – Torfi's marshes

Torfatindar and Torfatindur – Alternate ways of saying Torfi's peak. Tindar is specific to peaks formed in sub-glacial eruptions.

Tuddi – In consulting some Icelandic translation software, I received "Colby from Ohio". Let's go with it.

Tvíbaka - Double back

Útigönguhöfðar – The joy of hiking outdoors (seriously).

Vondugil – Wicked Valley

Glossary

Basalt – Lava or cinders produced from a mafic magma. Many lava flows and cinder cones in Iceland are basaltic in composition. Basaltic eruptions can be either explosive or effusive.

Bombs – Large gobs of molten lava launched from volcanic craters that travel on ballistic paths till they impact on the flanks of the volcano. As they fly, bombs cool to varying degrees resulting in different impact structures such as "breadcrust bombs" or "cow flop/pie bombs."

Caldera – Large crater resulting from huge eruptive events in which a large part of the overlying volcano collapses into the emptied magma chamber. Calderas can be many 10's of kilometers in diameter and are capable of creating "climate-changing" eruptions. Yellowstone is an example of a caldera.

Effusive – Passive in nature; non explosive, oozing of lava to the earth's surface.

Felsic – Term used to describe a high-viscosity magma or lava with a composition high in SiO_2. These materials generally produce explosive eruptions when they are gas-rich, or lava domes when gas-poor.

Fumaroles – Vents, specific to volcanic areas that expel warm to hot steam and other gasses. Some fumaroles are very high pressure and sound like jet engines. Others are more passive.

Hornito – Literally means "little oven" in Spanish, but it is the name for a small vent within a lava flow where bubbling due to degassing creates an accumulation cone of spattered lava around the vent.

Hyaloclastite – Eruptive product resulting from rising magma or lava encounter a large volume of water, ice, or snowpack. Deposits are usually welded together and have clasts of various sizes.

Jökulhlaup – Consider it a flash flood of concrete mix. When a sub-glacial volcano erupts, tons of ice is melted and immediately mobilized in a flash flood. As the water moves down slope it incorporates ash, rock and even boulders from within the drainage. These floods can travel upwards of 100km, destroying anything in their paths.

Lava - Molten to partially molten rock as it is found on the earth's surface.

Mafic – Term used to describe low-viscosity magma or lava with compositions low in SiO_2. These materials produce lava fountains or cinder cones when gas rich, or passive lava flows when gas-poor.

Magma – Molten to partially molten rock as it is found beneath the earth's surface.

Obsidian – A black glassy rock formed when lava cools extremely quickly.

Palagonite – Alteration product due to the interaction of water with volcanic glass of *mafic* composition.

Pillow Lava – Spherical deposit of basalt resulting from immediate quenching of lava by submersion within deep, standing water. Pillows have a distinct margin of chilled volcanic glass surrounding a more massive core. Most often, pillow are found associated with deep ocean volcanics.

Pyroclastic – *Pyro* is fire and *clastic* means rock. These are rocks, cinders, and ash that are thrown out of a volcanic crater during an eruption. They emerge very hot and cool while traveling through the air.

Rhyolite – Ash or lava produced from a felsic magma. Around Iceland, areas of rhyolite are commonly associated with highly explosive eruptions.

Surge – High-energy volcanic event where just enough water interacts with the magma to create an explosion. Surges are episodic, meaning they are discreet events separated by pauses of a few instants to several seconds or minutes.

Volcanic Explosivity Index (VEI) – This is like the Richter scale for volcanic eruptions. The VEI is based on the amount of material ejected by the eruption. The scale runs from 1-8. For perspective, Eyjafjallajökull (2010) was a 4; St Helens (1980) was a 5; Mount Pinatubo (1991) was a 6; and Yellowstone (640,000 ybp) was an 8.

Bibliography and Additional Suggested Reading

Björnsson, H., Pálsson F. and Gudmundsson, M.T., (2000) Surface and bedrock topography of the Mýrdalsjökull ice cap, Iceland. The Katla caldera, eruption sites and routes of jökulhlaups. Jökull 49.

Diamond, J, 2005, Collapse: New York, NY, Viking, 575 p.

Dugmore, A.J., Newton, A.J., Smith, K.T., and Mairs, K, (2013) Tephrachronology and the late Holocene volcanic and flood history of Eyjafjallajokull, Iceland. Journal of Quaternary Science 28(3): 237-247.

Handl, C and Handl, G, 2011, Iceland; The finest coastal and mountain walks: Munich, DE, Berverlag Rother, 141p.

Haraldsson Olafur Orn, 2011, Fjallabak Nature Reserve, Reykjavik, Eymundsson, 160 p.

Mangerud , J., Lie, S.V., Furned, H., Kristiansen, I.L., Lømo, L. (1984) A Younger Dryas Ash Bed in Western Norway, and Its Possible Correlations with Tephra in Cores from the Norwegian Sea and the North Atlantic. Quaternary Research 21:85-104.

Owen J, Tuffen H, McGarvie D., (2012) Using dissolved H (sub 2) O in rhyolitic glasses to estimate palaeo-ice thickness during a subglacial eruption at Blahnukur (Torfajokull, Iceland). *Bulletin Of Volcanology* 74(6):1355-1378.

Saemundsson, K. (2009) Torfajokull, Iceland – A rhyolite volcano and its geothermal resource. *Proceedings from Short Course III on Exploration for Geothermal Resources.* United Nations University, Lake Naivasha, Kenya. 11p.

Sigurdsson, Haraldur, (ed.), 2000, Encyclopedia of volcanoes: San Diego, CA, Academic Press, 1417 p.

32353834R00044

Made in the USA
Lexington, KY
16 May 2014